What You
Know A

THE
AMERICAN
FLAG

Fra: Hopkinson

What You Should Know About

THE AMERICAN FLAG

By Earl P. Williams, Jr.

Illustrations by
Les Prosser

Thomas Publications
Gettysburg, Pennsylvania

Library of Congress Catalog Card Number
87-61317
ISBN 0-939631-10-5

Printed in the United States of America
First printing, 1987
Second printing, 1988
Revised edition, 1989
Second revised edition, 1992

Library of Congress Cataloging-in-Publication Data

Williams, Earl P.
  What you should know about the American flag.

  Bibliography: p.
  Includes index.
  Summary: Traces the history and origins of the United States flag
discussing how some of the early flags and symbols of other coun
tries played a role in the creation of the United States flag. Als
discusses the flag's proper usage and display.
  [1. Flags--United States--History--Juvenile literature. 2. Unite
States--History--Juvenile literature. [1. Flags--United States]]
Prosser, Lester, ill. II. Title.
CR113.W65 1987   929.9'2'0973   87-6131

To My Family
and to
Francis Hopkinson,
Father of the Stars and Stripes

*And, as the last vessel
spread her canvas to the wind,
the Americans hoisted a most
superb and splendid ensign
on their battery....*

Midshipman Robert J. Barrett,
Royal Navy, upon seeing the
Star-Spangled Banner, September 14, 1814

Contents

List of Figures

Foreword

In 1989 we celebrated the 175th Anniversary of the Battle of Baltimore, commemorating the valiant American defense of Baltimore in 1814 that inspired young Francis Scott Key, held behind British lines, to write a poem that became our National Anthem. It is only fitting that Earl Williams' book, *What You Should Know About the American Flag,* should receive special notice. The story of The Star-Spangled Banner, as well as other memorable events in our history that helped shape our flag makes this volume especially worthwhile. Readers, young and old alike, will find Mr. Williams' accounts of the origins and history of the flag interesting. What better way to celebrate the bicentennial of the U.S. Constitution than by learning the story of our flag, which illustrates the beginnings of the great American experiment.

Scott S. Sheads
Park Ranger/Historian
National Park Service
Fort McHenry National Monument & Historic Shrine

Preface

When most Americans picture the first U.S. flag, a flag with 13 stars in a circle -- the so-called "Betsy Ross Flag" -- comes to mind. Surprisingly, such a flag design, if it even existed during the Revolutionary War, was hardly known at that time. What most of us learned in elementary school about the flag was based on the Betsy Ross legend or sketchy information, at best. Paintings of the Revolutionary War (several were painted in the 19th Century) have also led us astray. Emanuel Leutze's "George Washington Crossing the Delaware" is a classic example.

The ambiguities surrounding the early flag are partially due to the lack of meticulous record keeping by our Nation's early history makers. This, coupled with the myths and "media hype" stemming from our Nation's Centennial Celebration (1876), filled the void with faulty information that has since left an indelible mark on the public's mind. Only in the last few years has technology allowed us to verify or refute the authenticity of Revolutionary War-era flags that were presumed authentic.

Nevertheless, our flag's heritage is fascinating because it mirrors the important events and periods in American history. This book highlights that heritage for the young reader and the reader wishing brief but accurate information. Further information on the U.S. flag, including its proper usage and display, is located in the appendix.

A Word to Teachers

Several scholarly books have been written on the U.S. flag since the 19th Century, yet by and large, the public knows little about the history of our greatest national symbol. Therefore, I felt that a word to our teachers would be appropriate since they can effectively teach the flag's history to our future citizens.

Francis Hopkinson did not design the Stars and Stripes in a vacuum. Instead, his design was a modification of colonial British and American flags. Flag Day, June 14, offers a great opportunity for teaching this heritage. When handled conscientiously, pupils will understand the genesis of our flag's design and what the flag stands for. They will also understand that although our ties with Great Britain were severed politically, our kinship with the mother country was not totally abrogated. Discussing this relationship in class is important because our heritage as a nation was not formed in a vacuum, either. Our laws of today and the principles found in Jefferson's Declaration of Independence and Madison's Constitution can be traced to King John's Magna Charta of 1215. Certainly, these principles, along with our heterogeneous heritage, have made us the greatest nation on earth.

Teachers may also wish to contact flag historians (vexillologists). The Flag Research Center, Winchester, Mass.; the Division of Naval History, Museum of American History, Smithsonian Institution, Washington, D.C.; and the Naval Academy Museum, Annapolis, Md., have invaluable information to offer. Field trips to these locations are also a possibility.

Acknowledgements

First, I would like to thank Ms. Vera F. Rollo, historian and author, for the encouragement, assistance, and support that she has given me as a writer over the years. I would also like to thank the following individuals and institutions for their invaluable help in preparing this book: Mr. Gordon Bowen-Hassell, Historian, Historical Research Branch, Naval Historical Center, Washington Navy Yard; British Naval Staff, Washington, D.C.; Ms. Suzanne B. Brown, Audiovisual Librarian, The Colonial Williamsburg Foundation, Williamsburg, Va.; Ms. Barbara Chinn, Librarian, the Canadian Embassy, Washington, D.C.; Ms. Jane Collins, Reference Librarian, National Gallery of Art Library, Washington, D.C.; Mr. Dan Crawford, Historian, U.S. Marine Corps Historical Center, Washington Navy Yard; Mr. W.G. Crampton, Director, The Flag Institute, Chester, England; Department of Archives and History, State of Alabama, Montgomery, Ala.; the Embassy of Australia, Washington, D.C.; the Embassy of Ireland, Washington, D.C.; Ms. Merle Fabian, Head Librarian, the Canadian Embassy, Washington, D.C.; Mr. E.J. Grove, Deputy Head, Strategic Studies, Academic Department, Britannia Royal Naval College, Dartmouth, Devon, England; Mr. David C. Hahn, Curator of Collections, The Museum of the Confederacy, Richmond, Va.; Dr. Dane Hartgrove, Archivist, National Archives, Washington, D.C.; Ms. Angela Kilkenny, Librarian, the Canadian Embassy, Washington, D.C.; Mr. Donald Kloster, Associate Curator, Division of Military History, Museum of American History, Smithsonian Institution, Washington, D.C.; Dr. Opal Landrum, Institute of Heraldry, U.S. Army, Alexandria, Va.; Dr. Harold D. Langley, Curator of Naval History, Museum of American History, Smithsonian Institution, Washington, D.C.; Mr. Raymond Mann, Historian, Ships History Branch, Dudley Knox Center for Naval History, Washington Navy Yard; Ms. Linda Mayfield, Librarian, British Information Service, New York, N.Y.; Mr. Larry McDonald, Archivist/Consultant, National Archives, Washington, D.C.;

Ms. Marjorie Miller, Reference Librarian, Prince George's County Public Documents Reference Library, Upper Marlboro, Md.; Maryland Room, Hyattsville Branch, Prince George's County Memorial Library, Hyattsville, Md.; Music Division, Martin Luther King Memorial Library, Washington, D.C.; New Zealand Embassy, Washington, D.C.; Dr. Edward C. Papenfuse, State Archivist and Commissioner of Land Patents, Maryland State Archives, Annapolis, Md.; Mr. John Reilly, Historian, Ships History Branch, Dudley Knox Center for Naval History, Washington Navy Yard; Ms. Adel Richey, Institute of Heraldry, U.S. Army, Alexandria, Va.; Mr. Scott Sheads, Park Ranger/ Historian, National Park Service, Ft. McHenry National Monument and Historic Shrine, Baltimore Md.; Ms. Janet Shewbridge, Ft. McHenry National Monument and Historic Shrine, Baltimore, Md.; Dr. Whitney Smith, Director, The Flag Research Center, Winchester, Mass.; Ms. Florian H. Thayn, Head, Art and Reference Division, Architect of the Capitol, Washington, D.C.; Mr. Henry Vadnais, Navy Curator, Naval Historical Center, Washington Navy Yard; Mr. Ted Weir, Archivist/Consultant, National Archives, Washington, D.C.; Miss H.P. White, Naval Historical Library, Ministry of Defense, London, England; and Mrs. Susan D. Williams, Editor.

E.P.W.

Fig. 1, the Stars and Stripes

Introduction

How did our flag come to be? You may have asked yourself this question before. On the other hand, you probably know that our flag was created during the Revolutionary War, when the 13 original colonies struggled for their independence from Great Britain. You may also know that on June 14, 1777, the Continental Congress passed a resolution stating that our flag would contain 13 alternating red and white stripes, and 13 white stars on a blue *field* in the flag's upper left-hand corner, or *canton.*

Each year, we celebrate June 14 as Flag Day, the birthday of the Stars and Stripes. But the evolution of our flag goes further back in time than you probably imagined. Let's take a look at some of the early flags and symbols of other countries that played a role in the creation of our flag.

Fig. 2, Saint George's Cross

Saint George's Cross

Nearly a thousand years ago, many Christian countries in western Europe joined forces to regain the Holy Land from Moslem control. England was one of the European countries that participated in these crusades against the Moslems. English crusaders would often wear the red Cross of Saint George, England's patron saint, into battle.

Fig. 3, the St. George flag

The St. George Flag

By 1450, the red St. George's Cross on a white field had become England's national flag. English explorers to the New World brought the St. George flag to America in the 1500's.

Fig. 4, the St. Andrew flag

The St. Andrew Flag

Scotland, to the north of England, had a patron saint much earlier than England did. The cross of Scotland's patron saint, St. Andrew, became that country's national emblem in 1385. Over time, the white Cross of St. Andrew on a blue field became Scotland's national flag. As you can see, the Cross of St. Andrew is shaped like an X. An X-shaped cross is called a *saltire*.

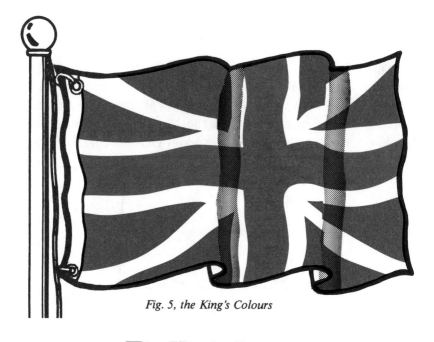

Fig. 5, the King's Colours

The King's Colours

Queen Elizabeth I of England had no heirs, so when she died in 1603, her cousin, King James VI of Scotland became the King of England also. As King of both England and Scotland, he was known as King James I. To show unity between the two countries, he decided to have the Scottish and English flags combined. The new flag was adopted on April 12, 1606, and was called the King's Colours. Twenty years later, this flag was given a new name -- the *Union* flag. As you can see, the Union flag was red, white, and blue. These colors were handed down to the United States flag during the Revolutionary War. The Union flag was brought to America when English settlers founded Jamestown, Virginia, in 1607.

The Union flag was primarily flown at sea. One of the three English ships that landed at Jamestown in 1607, the *Susan Constant,* flew the Union flag from the *mainmast* and the St. George flag from the *foremast.* On May 5, 1634, King Charles I -- King James' son -- decreed that only ships that were either in the Royal Navy or sailing for the Crown could fly the Union flag.

Sometimes, it was difficult to see a ship's flags because they flew at the top of the ship's tall masts, above the sails. The sails often obstructed a person's view of the flags, especially if the ship was sailing toward the person head-on. To remedy this problem, English and Scottish warships began flying a smaller Union flag at their *bows* so that they could be identified as warships head-on. This smaller flag was called the Union *Jack* because it was flown on the jack-*staff,* at the bow of the ship. But over time, people began calling the Union flag (which was larger than the Union Jack) the "Union Jack" also.

Here in the United States, the Union flag flies atop Williamsburg, Virginia's, restored Capitol building between July 5 and May 14. From May 15 to July 4, the Continental Colors, which will be discussed later, flies from the building.

Fig. 6, the Susan Constant and Godspeed

The Red Ensign

When Charles I became king in 1625, a special red flag called the Red *Ensign* was first flown at the *stern* of some English merchant ships. It carried the Cross of St. George on a white canton.

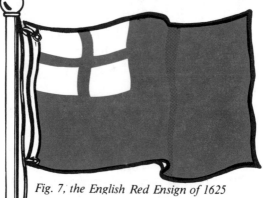

Fig. 7, the English Red Ensign of 1625

King Charles II, who came to the throne in 1660, officially allowed these ships to fly the Red Ensign in 1663. English merchant ships, therefore, could legally fly the Red Ensign from the stern and the St. George flag at the mainmast. But some ships broke the law and continued to fly the Union flag.

The Red Ensign came to America in the 1620's. It and its counterpart, the British Red Ensign of 1707, were very familiar to colonial Americans. The 1707 Ensign was flown in the colonies until and during the early stages of the Revolutionary War.

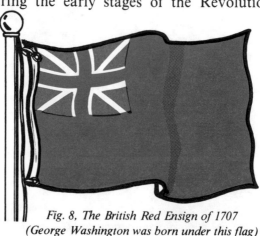

Fig. 8, The British Red Ensign of 1707
(George Washington was born under this flag)

In John Trumbull's painting entitled "Declaration of Independence," several British flags, including the Red Ensign, can be seen in the background hanging on a wall. These flags were captured from British forces during the Revolutionary War. Trumbull decided to put these flags in the painting; they may not have actually been on the wall. The painting hangs in the Rotunda of the U.S. Capitol in Washington, D.C.

Fig. 9, "Declaration of Independence" by John Trumbull
Architect of the Capitol

The Continental Navy Jack

The Red Ensign, the Continental Navy Jack, and other Revolutionary War-period flags played a major role in the creation of our flag. The Navy Jack's alternating red and white stripes signified the unity of the 13 colonies, and its rattlesnake warned the British monarchy not to abuse colonists' rights. The Navy Jack was adopted in 1775. This jack was similar to the South Carolina Navy ensign. The only difference was that the South Carolina ensign had red and blue alternating stripes.

Fig. 10, the Continental Navy Jack

*Fig. 11, the Continental Colors
(Williamsburg, Virginia)*

The First U.S. Flag

During the 1775/1776 winter, after the first shots of the War for Independence had been fired, American colonists adopted a new flag based on the British Red Ensign and other red- and white-striped flags. In fact, this new flag looked exactly like the British East India Company's flag. The new flag had several names; it was called The Continental Colors, The Grand Union Flag, The Cambridge Flag, and The Congress Flag.

On December 3, 1775, John Paul Jones (a Navy Lieutenant at the time) raised this flag aboard Captain Esek Hopkins' flagship the *Alfred.* Later, the flag was raised on the liberty pole at Prospect Hill on January 2, 1776. Prospect Hill was near George Washington's headquarters at Cambridge, Massachusetts.

The Continental Colors was our unofficial national flag on July 4, 1776, Independence Day. It was the unofficial national flag and ensign of the United States Navy until June 14, 1777.

The First Stars and Stripes

As previously mentioned, the first U.S. flag -- the Continental Colors -- was in use from December 3, 1775 to June 14, 1777, nearly 11 months after the colonies declared their independence from Great Britain. For almost a year after Independence Day, July 4, 1776, our national flag still carried the British Crosses of St. George and St. Andrew in the canton. Francis Hopkinson, a delegate to the Continental Congress from New Jersey and signer of the Declaration of Independence felt that we needed a new flag since we had broken away from Great Britain. Hopkinson became a member of the Marine Committee of the Continental Congress on July 12, 1776. On November 18 of that year, he became a member of the Navy Board, which reported to the Marine Committee.

Hopkinson felt that our Navy ships needed a new ensign and began designing a new flag with stars in the canton in place of the Crosses of St. George and St. Andrew. He probably got the idea for stars from his *coat of arms*. This design was accepted by Congress on June 14, 1777. On that day, Congress adopted the following resolution from its Marine Committee:

> *Resolved, That the Flag of the United States be thirteen stripes alternate red and white, that the Union be thirteen stars white on a blue field representing a new constellation.*

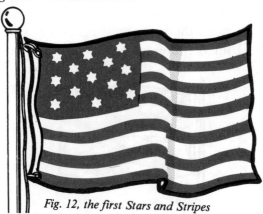

Fig. 12, the first Stars and Stripes

In 1780, Hopkinson asked Congress to reimburse him for designing the Stars and Stripes and other devices, including continental currency, the seal for the Admiralty Board, and the Great Seal of the United States. But the Treasury Board decided not to reimburse him because (1) he was not hired to make the designs, (2) he was already working for the government as a public servant, and (3) several other men were involved in designing the Great Seal. Since Hopkinson was not formally recognized for making these designs, most Americans do not know who he was.

The congressional resolution called for 13 stars in the flag's canton, but it did not specify how the stars would be arranged or how many points the stars would have. Some 13-star flags looked like the one shown in figure 12. Others looked like the flag shown in figure 13. Eight-pointed stars were the easiest to make. But by the early 1780's, some U.S. flags were being made with five-pointed stars. A five-pointed star is called a *mullet*. By the early 1800's, practically all U.S. flags had mullets instead of eight-pointed stars or six-pointed stars (called *estoiles*).

U.S. troops were accustomed to using their regimental *colors* during and after the Revolutionary War instead of the U.S. flag, thereby creating a very unique array. Except at forts, headquarters, and other buildings, the Army did not use the national flag in battle until the 1800's.

In the fall of 1781, British troops under General Charles Cornwallis surrendered to General Washington at Yorktown, Virginia, thus ending the Revolutionary War. Two years later, a peace treaty signed between the two countries at Paris officially ended the War. The United States was now an internationally recognized nation.

Fig. 13, the John Shaw Flag[1]

The 15-Star, 15-Stripe Flag and the Bombardment of Fort McHenry

By 1792, Vermont and Kentucky had joined the Union, and now there were 15 states. On May 1, 1795, Congress enacted the Second Flag Act to update the 13-star, 13-stripe U.S. flag. Congress decided to add two stars and **two stripes** to the new flag, which gave it 15 stars and 15 stripes. This flag was used in our second war with Great Britain, the War of 1812, even though there were 18 states in the Union when the War broke out! The three new states were Tennessee, Ohio, and Louisiana. (Congress did not update the 15-star flag until 1818.)

On August 19, 1814, British forces landed at Benedict, Maryland, and five days later attacked and burned Washington, D.C. Dr. William Beanes, an elderly friend of Francis Scott Key's, was taken prisoner and held aboard a British warship in the Chesapeake Bay. That September, Key, a Washington lawyer, was granted permission to board a prisoner-exchange vessel to intercede with British authorities for Beanes' release.

After burning Washington, the British planned to attack Baltimore, Maryland. But in order to do this, they would have to launch a naval attack against Baltimore's Fort McHenry first.

The British began the bombardment at dawn on Tuesday, September 13. It was only supposed to take two hours but lasted for 24 hours. The British ships could not get close enough to the Fort to get accurate aim. The low walls of the Fort made it a difficult target, and the Fort's guns kept the ships from getting within two miles of the Fort.

Key's prisoner-exchange vessel was anchored eight miles from the Fort at Old Roads Bay, which is on the Patapsco River. Key was too far away from the Fort to see it or the Fort's flag with his naked eye or even a telescope. Furthermore, the 16 British ships in the water between his ship and the Fort, the stormy weather, and the smoke from the cannon fire obstructed his view.

On the following morning, Key awoke to find that the British *task force* was retreating; the attack had failed. The Fort's 15-star,

15-stripe *storm flag,* which had flown throughout the bombardment and the stormy night, was lowered as the Fort's *garrison* celebrated and raised the Fort's 15-star, 15-stripe *garrison flag.* This was the flag that Key saw through a telescope on the morning of September 14, 1814, after the British released him and he sailed toward Baltimore. Francis Scott Key called the flag the "Star-Spangled Banner."

The Fort's garrison flag was the largest one in the world at the time. It measured 42 feet by 30 feet and weighed about 90 pounds. Twelve men were required to raise the flag. Mary Young Pickersgill, a flag maker who lived in Baltimore, and her daughter Caroline sewed the Fort's garrison flag and storm flag a year before the battle. The garrison flag was so large that they had to finish it on the floor of the local brewery!

Upon seeing the garrison flag, Key, an amateur poet, was so elated that he immediately began composing a poem about the bombardment. Entitled by newspapers "The Defense of Ft. McHenry," it was later changed to "The Star-Spangled Banner." Key borrowed a popular English tune for it to be sung by. Although the "Star-Spangled Banner" was used as our unofficial National Anthem starting in the mid-1800's, it did not become our official National Anthem until March 3, 1931.

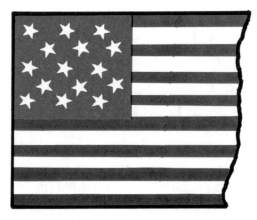

Fig. 14, the Original Star-Spangled Banner

If you ever go to the Smithsonian Institution in Washington, D.C., to see the original Star-Spangled Banner, you may wonder why the flag is so torn. As we have just seen, the flag that Key saw did not fly throughout the bombardment and, hence, was not shot at. When Ft. McHenry's commander, Colonel George Armistead retired, he took the Star-Spangled Banner with him. Afterwards, the flag was handed down to his descendents, who cut off pieces of the flag as souvenirs. This is why the flag is so torn at its *fly* end. In Baltimore, a 15-star, 15-stripe flag flies at the Fort by Presidential orders.

We sing "The Star-Spangled Banner" at the beginning of all major sports events. Playing the National Anthem at ball games started during the seventh-inning stretch of the opening game of the 1918 World Series. The First World War was just about over. Thereafter, the National Anthem was played not only at the World Series, but at the opening game of the baseball season as well. Playing the National Anthem before all ball games became customary during World War II. A 15-star, 15-stripe flag flies at Baltimore's Memorial Stadium.

Fig. 15, Francis Scott Key

National Portrait Gallery, Smithsonian Institution

"The Star-Spangled Banner"

by Francis Scott Key, September 1814
(Sung to the tune "To Anacreon in Heaven")

Oh! say, can you see, by the dawn's early light,
What so proudly we hailed at the twilight's last gleaming?
Whose broad stripes and bright stars, thro' the perilous fight,
O'er the ramparts we watched were so gallantly streaming?
And the rockets' red glare, the bombs bursting in air,
Gave proof thro' the night that our flag was still there.
Oh! say, does that star-spangled banner yet wave
O'er the land of the free and the home of the brave?

On the shore, dimly seen thro' the mist of the deep,
Where the foe's haughty host in dread silence reposes,
What is that which the breeze, o'er the towering steep,
As it fitfully blows, half conceals, half discloses?
Now it catches the gleam of the morning's first beam,
In full glory reflected, now shines on the stream.
'Tis the star-spangled banner. Oh! long may it wave
O'er the land of the free and the home of the brave.

And where is that band who so vauntingly swore
That the havoc of war and the battle's confusion
A home and a country should leave us no more?
Their blood has washed out their foul footsteps pollution.
No refuge could save the hireling and slave
From the terror of flight or the gloom of the grave,
And the star-spangled banner in triumph doth wave
O'er the land of the free and the home of the brave.

Oh! thus be it ever when freemen shall stand
Between their loved home and war's desolation,
Blest with vict'ry and peace, may the Heav'n-rescued land
Praise the Pow'r that hath made and preserved us a nation.
Then conquer we must, when our cause it is just,
And this be our motto, "In God is our trust."
And the star-spangled banner in triumph shall wave
O'er the land of the free and the home of the brave.

Fig. 16. a 20-Star flag

Back to 13 Stripes

By 1818, 20 states had been admitted to the Union, but no stars or stripes had been added to the flag since the 15th state. Congress realized that adding stripes to the flag for each new state would make the flag look awkward. So, on April 4, 1818, Congress finally determined that the flag would contain only 13 red and white stripes for the 13 original states. However, a new star would be added to the canton for each new state on the 4th of July following the state's admission.

Fig. 17, the Fort Sumter Flag

The Fort Sumter Flag

Our Nation's greatest crisis, the Civil War, raised a perplexing question for the U.S. flag. With the Southern states leaving the Union to form their own country, the Confederate States of America, should the stars in the U.S. flag representing those states be removed? President Lincoln's answer to this question was "No." He felt that the Union could never be dissolved. In fact, three stars were added to the flag for Kansas (34th state), West Virginia (35th state), and Nevada (36th state) between 1861 and 1865, when the War ended.

Hostilities broke out between the United States and the Confederacy in April 1861, when the Confederate forces under General Pierre Gustave Toutant de la Beauregard fired on U.S. troops stationed in Charleston, South Carolina, at Fort Sumter. President Lincoln had sent supplies there to U.S. Major Robert Anderson's stranded troops, who resisted South Carolina's secession from the Union. But the Fort was overwhelmed and surrendered on April 14, 1861. Major Anderson was permitted to evacuate his troops and take the Fort's garrison flag north. The Fort Sumter Flag had 33 stars. The original flag may be seen today on display at the Fort.

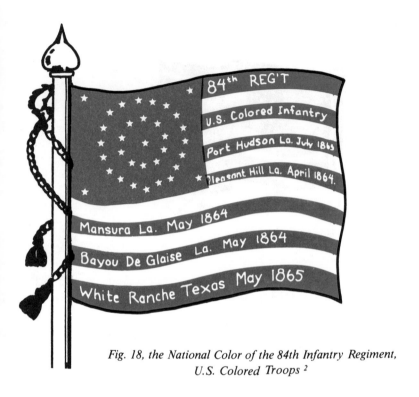

Fig. 18, the National Color of the 84th Infantry Regiment,
U.S. Colored Troops [2]

National Color of the 84th Infantry Regiment, United States Colored Troops

Negro slavery in the Southern states and ensuing arguments over it between the North and South contributed heavily to the War. On January 1, 1863, President Lincoln issued a proclamation to the Confederate States. It set the slaves in the Confederacy free and was known as the Emancipation Proclamation. Soon afterwards, the U.S. Army began recruiting blacks to fight for the Union. All-black Army units entitled the United States Colored Troops were established for this purpose. In addition, the Navy also recruited blacks. The flag shown above is on display at the Museum of American History, Smithsonian Institution. It is the national color of the 84th Infantry Regiment, United States Colored Troops.

The Legend of Barbara Frietchie

The Civil War stirred up patriotic feelings in the North and the South, and each side had patriotic songs and poems dedicated to their cause. The North's most popular song was "The Battle Hymn of the Republic," and the most popular Southern song was "Dixie." Abolitionist John Greenleaf Whittier wrote a poem about a legendary heroine of Frederick, Maryland, who defiantly flew her U.S. flag in view of Confederate General Thomas J. "Stonewall" Jackson and his men. The setting for Whittier's poem was September 1862 just before the crucial Battle of Antietam (near Sharpsburg, Md.), but there is no proof that Barbara Frietchie did these things.

Fig. 19, the Legend of Barbara Frietchie

Up from the meadows rich with corn,
Clear in the cool September morn,

The clustered spires of Frederick stand
Green-walled by the hills of Maryland.

Round about them orchards sweep,
Apple and peach tree fruited deep,

Fair as the garden of the Lord
To the eyes of the famished rebel horde,

On that pleasant morn of the early fall
When Lee marched over the mountain wall;

Over the mountains winding down,
Horse and foot, into Frederick town.

Forty flags with their silver stars,
Forty flags with their crimson bars,

Flapped in the morning wind: the sun
Of noon looked down, and saw not one.

Up rose old Barbara Frietchie then,
Bowed with her fourscore years and ten;

Bravest of all in Frederick town,
She took up the flag the men hauled down.

In her attic window the staff she set,
To show that one heart was loyal yet.

Up the street came the rebel tread,
Stonewall Jackson riding ahead.

Under his slouched hat left and right
He glanced; the old flag met his sight.

"Halt!" -- the dust-brown ranks stood fast.
"Fire!" -- out blazed the rifle-blast.

It shivered the window, pane and sash;
It rent the banner with seam and gash.

Quick, as it fell, from the broken staff
Dame Barbara snatched the silken scarf.

She leaned far out on the window-sill,
And shook it forth with a royal will.

"Shoot, if you must, this old gray head,
But spare your country's flag," she said.

A shade of sadness, a blush of shame,
Over the face of the leader came;

The nobler nature within him stirred
To life at that woman's deed and word;

"Who touches a hair of yon gray head
Dies like a dog! March on!" he said.

All day long through Frederick street
Sounded the tread of marching feet:

All day long that free flag tost
Over the heads of the rebel host.

Ever its torn folds rose and fell
On the loyal winds that loved it well;

And through the hill-gaps sunset light
Shone over it with a warm good-night.

Barbara Frietchie's work is o'er,
And the Rebel rides on his raids no more.

Honor to her! and let a tear
Fall, for her sake, on Stonewall's bier.

Over Barbara Frietchie's grave,
Flag of Freedom and Union, wave!

Peace and order and beauty draw
Round thy symbol of light and law;

And ever the stars above look down
On thy stars below in Frederick town! [3]

Fig. 20, the So-Called "Betsy Ross Flag" [4]

Our Country's Centennial and Other Patriotic Anniversaries Created Confusion Over the Flag's Early History

Many Americans believe that Betsy Ross, a seamstress who lived in Philadelphia, Pennsylvania, during the Revolutionary War, sewed the first Stars and Stripes. The flag that they think of had 13 five-pointed stars arranged in a circle. Some even think that this type of flag was the first U.S. flag. But as we saw earlier, the first U.S. flag was the Continental Colors -- a flag which still carried the Crosses of St. George and St. Andrew in the canton.

The reason most Americans believe that Betsy Ross sewed the first Stars and Stripes is due to the efforts of her grandson, William Canby. In 1870, six years before our country's Centennial, he told members of the Pennsylvania Historical Society that General George Washington and members of a congressional committee visited Mrs. Ross and asked her to sew the first Stars and Stripes.

According to the story, the meeting took place in June 1776 -- a month before the colonies declared their independence from Great Britain, and one whole year before Congress adopted the Stars and Stripes as our national flag. Mrs. Ross was 24 years old at the time. She supposedly told the committee that she could make the flag and, in the process, sew five-pointed stars as easily as six-pointed ones.

Mr. Canby said that his grandmother told him this story when he was a small boy. He secured affidavits from many relatives, several of whom worked with Mrs. Ross, to support the story. Pretty soon, Americans began to believe the story, and artists began to paint the U.S. flag with 13 stars in a circle in paintings of the Revolutionary War.

There is no proof that the meeting between Betsy Ross and George Washington ever took place. There are no records or receipts showing that Mrs. Ross sewed this type of flag, and the congressional committee that supposedly accompanied General Washington never existed. Mrs. Ross did sew flags for 50 years. Unfortunately, we do not know what they looked like. We do know that on May 29, 1777, she was paid for making flags for the Pennsylvania State Navy.

The first known example of a U.S. flag with 13 stars arranged in a circle dates from 1792, 13 years after Congress adopted the Flag Resolution. During the Revolution, power machinery had not been introduced, and it was much harder to sew stars on a flag in a perfect circle than to paint them in a circle. Therefore, artists were hired to paint the stars on flags of this nature.

During the War of 1812, the 27th Maryland Regiment used a flag with 12 stars arranged in a circle and one star in the center. This flag had seven red and six white stripes. Later, people thought that this flag was used in the Revolution.

In 1834, two years after the centennial anniversary of George Washington's birth, Army artillery units started using the Stars and Stripes as a national color. Some of these flags had 13 stars arranged in a circle. This type of flag was also used in the Mexican War (1842), when the Army infantry began using the Stars and Stripes as a national color.[5] By 1876, America's Centennial, people who did not know otherwise felt that these were also Revolutionary War flags. But as we have seen earlier, the first Stars and Stripes flags usually had their stars staggered in horizontal rows of 3-2-3-2-3 or 4-5-4, and the stars had six or eight points.

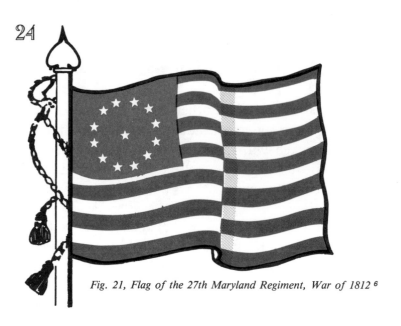

Fig. 21, Flag of the 27th Maryland Regiment, War of 1812 [6]

Fig. 22, U.S. Army Cavalry Guidon, Civil War

The 48-Star Flag

In 1912, Arizona, the 48th and last of the continental states, came into the Union. Now, the United States stretched from the Atlantic to the Pacific -- from "sea to shining sea." On October 29, 1912, President William Howard Taft issued an Executive Order which prescribed the flag's proportions and referred to the size and position of the stars. A joint board of Army and Navy officers influenced President Taft to issue the Executive Order. Patriotic groups were also especially interested in the flag at this time. They wanted national laws that would ensure proper respect for the flag. Although the Order was withdrawn shortly thereafter, President Woodrow Wilson reinstated it in 1916.

The 48-star flag was used in the United States longer than any other U.S. flag. It lasted from 1912 to 1959, when Alaska became the 49th state. The 48-star flag saw the United States emerge as a world power. It was the flag which the United States fought under in the First World War. It was the flag which flew over our country during our Nation's bleakest period since the Civil War -- the Great Depression. And it was the flag which saw the United States through the Japanese bombing of Pearl Harbor, the Second World War, and the Korean War.

Probably the most dramatic image of the 48-star flag was taken by photographer Joe Rosenthal on Iwo Jima during the Second World War. With support from the Navy, U.S. Marines invaded the tiny Pacific island between February and March of 1945 in order to establish an air base from which U.S. planes could attack Japan. Japan had heavily fortified the island and used it as an air base. Fighting was intense, and thousands of Marines lost their lives in capturing the island. Although the U.S. flag was raised on Iwo Jima on February 23, the island did not fall under U.S. control until March 16, 1945.

A statue of the five brave Marines and Navy corpsman who raised the 48-star flag at Iwo Jima stands in Arlington, Virginia, near Arlington National Cemetery. One of the five Marines, PFC Ira H. Hayes, was a Pima Indian from Arizona.

Fig. 23, the Flag Raising at Iwo Jima
National Archives

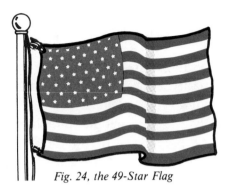

Fig. 24, the 49-Star Flag

The 49-Star Flag

The 49-star flag was one of America's shortest-lived flags; it only lasted for one year (July 4, 1959, to July 4, 1960). This flag represented Alaska's admission to the Union. On July 4, 1960, the 50th star was added to the U.S. flag for the state of Hawaii.

Fig. 25, the 50-Star Flag

The 50-Star Flag

The 50-star flag is our current flag. Like the 48-star flag, the 50-star flag has also seen many historical events. It has witnessed the Civil Rights Movement of the 1960's and the War in Vietnam. It was raised on the moon by our astronauts on July 20, 1969 (no other country has landed a person on the moon), and it witnessed a joyous time for all Americans -- the celebration of our country's 200th birthday on July 4, 1976. And, of course, the 50-star flag is witnessing today's history in the making.

What Our Flag Represents

The United States flag represents what our country stands for -- liberty, justice, equality, and opportunity -- at home, on the seas, and abroad. Our country was created with a dream in mind -- that Americans could live as free people and that Americans could achieve their highest potential if they wanted to. But in order for our country to live up to its creed, we ourselves must do likewise. By abiding by the principles found in our Declaration of Independence and Constitution, upholding our laws and changing them when they need to be changed, gaining knowledge, and being productive citizens, we are keeping our Nation the greatest on earth. Therefore, we must all be aware of what the United States stands for, and we must take an interest in our country. Otherwise, the principles that our country stands for will fade away like the colors of a weather-worn flag.

Fig. 26, The Stars and Stripes

APPENDIX

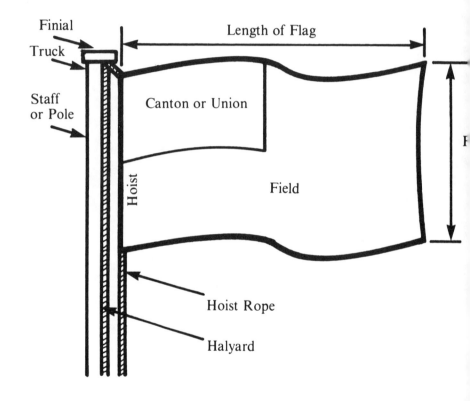

Fig. A-1, parts of a flag.

Fig. A-2, The Commissioning Pennant

*The commissioning pennant, flown at the masthead, is the
distinguishing mark of a commissioned naval ship.*

The U.S. Union Jack

The U.S. Union Jack, sometimes called the Navy Jack, is the
only variant of the U.S. flag used today. It has 50 stars on a blue
field and is essentially the canton of the U.S. flag. It flies at the
bow of anchored naval ships from 8:00 a.m. (0800 hours in military time) to sunset.

*Fig. A-3, the U.S. Union Jack
(the U.S.S. New Jersey, BB-62)*

Executive Order.

The Executive Order of June 24, 1912, is hereby revoked, and for it is substituted the following:

Whereas, "An Act to Establish the Flag of the United States", approved on the 4th of April, 1818, reading as follows:

"SECTION 1. Be it enacted, etc., That from and after the fourth day of July next, the flag of the United States be thirteen horizontal stripes, alternate red and white; that the union have twenty stars, white in a blue field.

"SECTION 2. Be it further enacted, That on the admission of every new State into the Union, one star be added to the union of the flag; and that such addition shall take effect on the fourth of July next, succeeding such admission."

fails to establish proportions; and

Whereas, investigation shows some sixty-six different sizes of National flags, and of varying proportions, in use in the Executive Departments;

It is hereby ordered that National Flags and Union Jacks for all Departments of the Government, with the exception noted under (a), shall conform to the following proportions:

Hoist (width) of Flag	1
Fly (length) of Flag	1.9
Hoist (width) of Union	7/13
Fly (length) of Union	.76
Width of each stripe	1/13

(a) Exception: The colors carried by troops, and camp colors, shall be the sizes prescribed for the Military Service (Army and Navy).

Limitation of the number of sizes: With exception of colors under note (a), the sizes of flags manufactured or purchased for Government Departments will be limited to those with the following hoists.

(1)	20 feet
(2)	19 feet (standard)
(3)	14.35 feet
(4)	12.19 feet
(5)	10 feet
(6)	8.94 feet
(7)	5.14 feet
(8)	5 feet
(9)	3.52 feet
(10)	2.90 feet
(11)	2.37 feet
(12)	1.31 feet

Union Jacks: The size of the Jack shall be the size of the Union of the National Flag with which it is flown.

Position and Size of Stars: The position and size of each star for the Union of the flag shall be as indicated on a plan which will be furnished to the Departments by the Navy Department. From this plan can be determined the location and size of stars for flags of any dimensions. Extra blueprints of this plan will be furnished upon application to the Navy Department.

Order effective: All National Flags and Union Jacks now on hand or for which contracts have been awarded shall be continued in use until unserviceable, but all those manufactured or purchased for Government use after the date of this order shall conform strictly to the dimensions and proportions herein prescribed.

Boat Flags: In order that the identity of the stars in flags when carried by small boats belonging to the Government may be preserved, the custom holding in the Navy for many years, of thirteen (13) stars for boat flags, is hereby approved.

President's Flag: The color of the field of the President's flag shall be blue.

WM H TAFT

THE WHITE HOUSE,
October 29, 1912.

[No. 1637]

Pledge of Allegiance to the Flag

The Pledge of Allegiance was written in Boston in connection with the 400th anniversary of America's discovery, October 12, 1892. After slight modifications, Congress officially approved the Pledge on June 22, 1942, and on June 14, 1954 (Flag Day), the phrase "under God" was added.

"I pledge allegiance to the Flag
of the United States of America,
and to the Republic for which it stands,
one Nation under God, indivisible,
with liberty and justice for all."

(Pub. L. 94-344, July 7, 1976, 90 Stat. 813.)

How to Display the Flag [7]

Laws have been written to govern the use of the flag and to insure a proper respect for the Stars and Stripes. Custom has decreed certain other observances in regard to its use.

All the Services have precise regulations regarding the display of the National flag, which may vary somewhat from the general rules below.

Respect your flag and render it the courtesies to which it is entitled by observing the following rules:

The National flag should be raised and lowered by hand. Do not raise the flag while it is furled. Unfurl, then hoist quickly to the top of the staff. Lower it slowly and with dignity. Place no objects on or over the flag. A speaker's table is sometimes covered with the flag. This practice should be avoided.

When displayed in a church or public auditorium, the flag should be placed on a staff at the clergyman's or speaker's right as he or she faces the audience. Any other flag so displayed should be placed on the left of the clergyman or speaker. [Taken from U.S. Code, Chapter 10, Sec. 175(k); Pub. L. 94-344, July 7, 1976, 90 Stat. 810.]

1. When displayed over the middle of the street, the flag should be suspended vertically with the union to the north in an east and west street, or to the east in a north and south street. [See fig. A-4.]

2. When displayed with another flag from crossed staffs, the flag of the United States of America should be on the right (the flag's own right) and its staff should be in front of the staff of the other flag. [See fig. A-5.]

3. When it is to be flown at half-mast, the flag should be hoisted to the peak for an instant and then lowered to the half-mast position; but before lowering the flag for the day it should again be raised to the peak. By half-mast is meant hauling down the

flag to one-half the distance between the top and the bottom of the staff. On Memorial Day display at half-mast until noon only; then hoist to the top of staff. [See fig. A-6.]

4. When flags of states or cities or pennants of societies are flown on the same hoist rope with the flag of the United States of America, the latter should always be at the peak. When flown from adjacent staffs the Stars and Stripes should be hoisted first and lowered last. [See fig. A-7.]

5. When the flag is suspended over a sidewalk from a rope extending from house to pole at the edge of the sidewalk, the flag should be hoisted out from the building, toward the pole, union first. [See fig. A-8.]

6. When the flag is displayed from a staff projecting horizontally or at any angle from the window sill, balcony, or front of a building, the union of the flag should go to peak at the staff (unless the flag is to be displayed at half-mast). [See fig. A-9.]

Fig. A-4

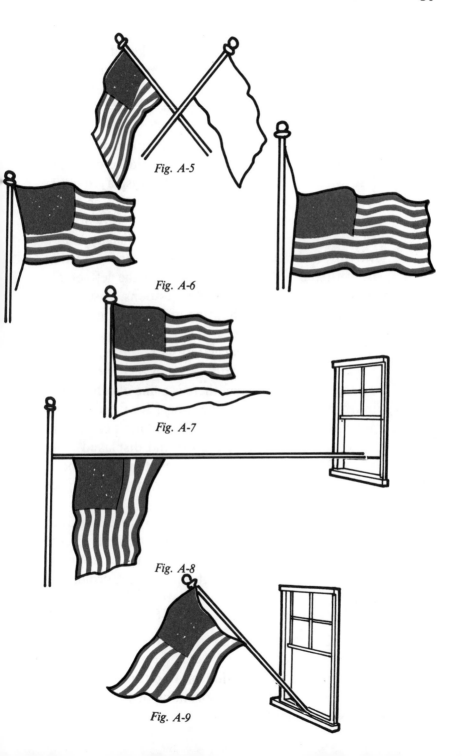

Fig. A-5

Fig. A-6

Fig. A-7

Fig. A-8

Fig. A-9

7. When the flag is used to cover a casket, it should be so placed that the union is at the head and over the left shoulder. The flag should not be lowered into the grave or allowed to touch the ground. [See fig. A-10.]

8. When the flag is displayed in a manner other than by being flown from a staff, it should be displayed flat, whether indoors or out. When displayed either horizontally or vertically against a wall, the union should be uppermost and to the flag's own right, that is, to the observer's left. When displayed in a window it should be displayed in the same way, that is, with the union or blue field to the left of the observer in the street. When festoons, rosettes or drapings are desired, bunting of blue, white and red should be used, but never the flag. [See fig. A-11.]

9. When carried in a procession with another flag or flags, the Stars and Stripes should be either on the marching right, or when there is a line of other flags, in front of the center of that line. [See fig. A-12.]

10. When a number of flags of states or cities or pennants of societies are grouped and displayed from staffs with our National flag, the latter should be at the center or at the highest point of the group. [See fig. A-13.]

11. When the flags of two or more nations are displayed they should be flown from separate staffs of the same height, and the flags should be of approximately equal size. International usage forbids the display of the flag of one nation above that of another nation in time of peace. [See fig. A-14.]

The flag should never be displayed with the union down except as a signal of dire distress.

Do not use the flag as a portion of a costume or athletic uniform.[8] Do not embroider it upon cushions or handkerchiefs nor print it on paper napkins or boxes.

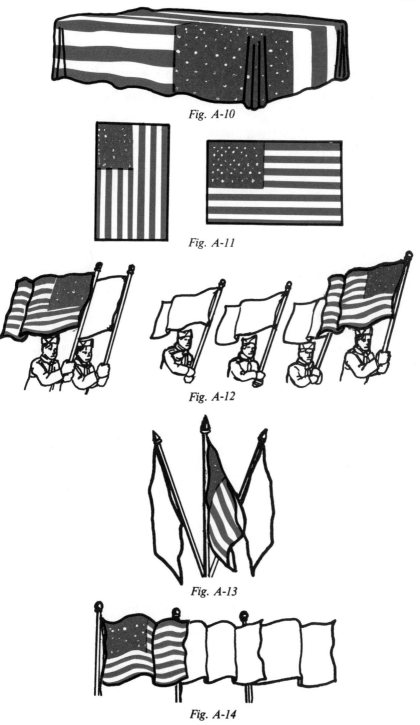

Fig. A-10

Fig. A-11

Fig. A-12

Fig. A-13

Fig. A-14

A federal law provides that a trademark cannot be registere which consists of, or comprises among other things, "the fla coat-of-arms or other insignia of the United States, or any simula tion thereof."

When the flag is used in unveiling a statue or monument, should not serve as a covering of the object to be unveiled. If it i displayed on such occasions, do not allow the flag to fall to th ground, but let it be carried aloft to form a feature of th ceremony.

Take every precaution to prevent the flag from becomin soiled. It should not be allowed to touch the ground or floor, no brush against objects.

The flag should not be dipped to any person or thing, with on exception: Navy vessels, upon receiving a salute of this type fror a vessel registered by a nation formally recognized by the Unite States, must return the compliment. This is called dipping th colors.

When carried, the flag should always be aloft and free -- neve flat or horizontal.

Never use the flag as drapery of any sort whatsoever. Buntin of blue, white, and red -- arranged with the blue above, the whit in the middle, and the red below -- should be used for suc purposes of decoration as covering a speaker's desk or draping th front of a platform.

Do not use the flag as a receptacle for receiving, holding, carry ing or delivering anything. Never place upon the flag, or attach t it, any mark, insignia, letter, work, figure, design, picture, o drawing of any nature.

No other flag may be flown above the Stars and Stripes, except (1) the United Nations flag at U.N. Headquarters; (2) the churc pennant, a dark blue cross on a white background, during churc services conducted by naval chaplains at sea.[9]

Notes

1

John Shaw, a cabinet maker of Annapolis, Maryland, made a flag of this design for the Continental Congress when Annapolis was our Nation's Capital (Dec. 1783 - June 1784). A replica of this flag can be seen in the Maryland State House, at Annapolis.

2

The following narrative accompanies the flag display:

"Originally the 12 Corps de Afrique, the 84th Regiment was formed in Port Hudson, Louisiana on April 14, 1864. The unit participated in numerous campaigns in Louisiana and Texas. In accordance with army regulations, the regimental designation and battle honors are painted on the flag. [No inscriptions, etc., were allowed on the U.S. flag after World War I.]"

"As was the case with most black units the commissioned officers of the 84th were white, and the Adjutant of the Regiment, Ustick O. Krause, maintained custody of the flag after his discharge. It remained a treasured possession of his family until 1982 when they donated the flag to the Smithsonian."

3

John Greenleaf Whittier, *The Complete Poetical Works of Whittier,* ed. Horace E. Scudder (Boston: Houghton, Mifflin & Co., 1894), pp. 342-343.

4

This 13-star flag may not have been used until 1792.

5

The Marine Corps began using the Stars and Stripes as a national color in 1876, and the U.S. Cavalry began using it as a national *standard* in 1887.

6

This flag was mistaken to have been the national color of the Third Maryland Regiment (Revolutionary War). The national flag at this time had 15 white stars in rows of 3-3-3-3-3 and 15 stripes.

7

Taken from *How to Respect and Display Our Flag,* NAVMC 6915 (Washington: U.S. Government Printing Office, 1968), pp. 26-30.

[8]
Flag patches may be worn on the uniforms of military personnel, firefighters, police officers, and members of patriotic organizations. See Title 4, U.S. Code, Chapter 10, Sec. 176(j).

[9]
For in-depth information regarding the display and usage of the U.S. flag, see Title 4, U.S. Code, Chapter 1, Sec. 1-3; Title 36, U.S. Code, Chapter 9, Sec. 141-162, Chapter 10, Sec. 170-178, Proc. No. 2605, Feb. 18, 1944, 9 F.R. 1957, 58 Stat. 1126; and Title 38 U.S. Code, Chapter 23, Sec. 901.

Glossary

BANNER — A rectangular flag used by a king, prince, duke, or other noble. The coat of arms of the owner covers the banner's entire surface. The term is also loosely applied to a national flag (e.g., the "Star-Spangled Banner").

BOW — The forward section of a ship.

CANTON — The quarters of a flag, especially the top quarter of the hoist.

COAT OF ARMS — The armorial and/or other heraldic badges of an owner displayed on a cloak or shield.

COLORS — The national and regimental or armorial flags carried by dismounted organizations (such as a color guard). Hence, the national color for Army and Marine Corps regiments is the U.S. flag. The term also applies to the national ensign flown aboard a naval vessel.

ENSIGN — A special flag based on a country's national flag and used exclusively on naval ships or merchant ships. The civil ensign is the merchant marine's flag. The U.S. flag serves as national flag, naval ensign, and civil ensign. Great Britain, on the other hand, has a white ensign for naval ships, a red ensign for merchant ships, and a blue ensign for merchant ships commanded by an officer in the Naval Reserve. Great Britain also has an ensign for the Royal Air Force and one for airports.

ESTOILE — A six-pointed, usually wavy, star.

FIELD — The ground of each division of a flag.

FLY — The edge of a flag farthest from the staff.

FOREMAST — The mast nearest the bow of a sailing ship.

GARRISON — A military installation, such as a fort. Also, the troops stationed there.

GARRISON FLAG — A large U.S. flag flown at forts. During the War of 1812, garrison flags were 20 feet by 40 feet. The Star-Spangled Banner measured 30 feet by 42 feet.

HALYARD — The rope by which a flag is raised on a flagpole.

HOIST — (n.) The edge of a flag nearest the staff. (vb.) To raise a flag.

HOIST ROPE — The rope on which a flag is flown on a flagpole.

JACK — A flag flown at the bow of warships when anchored. Great Britain's jack -- the British Union Jack -- combines the Crosses of St. George, St. Andrew, and St. Patrick on a blue field. The U.S. Union Jack carries 50 white stars on a blue field (the canton of the Naval Ensign). According to U.S. Navy regulations, the U.S. Union Jack should be the same size as the canton of the Naval Ensign flown at the ship's stern.

MAINMAST — The principal mast of a sailing ship.

MULLET — A five-pointed star, representative of a knight's spur.

SALTIRE — An x-shaped cross.

SHIP OF THE LINE — in the days of sail, a naval ship that fought in the line of battle.

STAFF — A small pole from which a flag is flown.

STANDARD — A flag which is colored according to the owner's livery and displays the owner's badge or badges instead of his arms. The term "national standard" is used to describe the national and regimental flags carried by mounted or motorized organizations.

STERN — The rear of a ship.

STORM FLAG — The U.S. flag which is flown at military installations during inclement weather. It is smaller than the U.S. flag that is usually flown at the installation (the post flag).

TASK FORCE — A group of naval ships such as a squadron, several squadrons, or a fleet with a specific military objective to accomplish.

UNION — A flag or device of a flag symbolizing the union of countries or states. Also, the canton of (1) the U.S. flag, (2) British ensigns, and (3) British Commonwealth flags that are based on the British ensigns.

Bibliography

Agay, Denes. *Best Loved Songs of the American People.* Garden City, N.Y.: Doubleday & Company, Inc., 1975.

Aikman, Lonnelle. "New Stars for Old Glory," *The National Geographic Magazine*, Vol. CXVI, No. 1 (July 1959), pp. 86-121.

Australian Department of Administrative Services. *The Australian National Flag.* Canberra: Australian Government Publishing Service, 1982.

Balderston, Lloyd. *The Evolution of the American Flag.* Philadelphia: Ferris & Leach, 1909.

Board of County Commissioners, Prince George's County. *1969 Annual Report to the People: Prince George's County, Maryland.* August 1969.

Boorstin, Daniel J. *The Americans: The Colonial Experience.* New York: Alfred A. Knopf, Inc., and Random House, Inc. (Vintage Books), 1958.

British Information Services, "The British Flag and Royal Coat of Arms" (fact sheet), Norwich, England: Soman-Wherry Press, Ltd., 1975.

"By the Queen, a Proclamation," *The Boston News-Letter* (Mon., Jan. 19 to Mon., Jan. 26, 1707), p.1.

Cayley, Frank. *Flag of Stars.* Melbourne: Rigby Group, 1966.

Chapman, Charles F. *Chapman Piloting: Seamanship and Small Boat Handling.* 54th ed. New York: Hearst Books, 1979.

Chestney, M. Jemison. *The History of the Confederate Flags.* Macon, Ga.: Jemison Chestney, 1925.

Christie, I.R. *Crisis of Empire: Great Britain and the American Colonies, 1754-1783.* New York: W.W. Norton & Company, Inc., 1966.

Clark, Patrick. *Sports Firsts.* New York: Facts on File, Inc., 1981.

Cooper, Grace. *Thirteen-Star Flags*. Washington: Smithsonian Institution Press, 1973.

Crampton, William. *The Observer's Book of Flags*. London: Frederick Waine, Ltd., 1979.

Eggenberger, David. *Flags of the U.S.A.* New York: Thomas Y. Crowell Co., 1964.

Executive Order No. 1637. October 29, 1912.

Furlong, William Rea and Byron McCandless. *So Proudly We Hail: The History of the United States Flag*. Washington: Smithsonian Institution Press, 1981.

Hanan, Sara B. and Edward C. Papenfuse. *The Maryland State House, Annapolis*. Prepared by the Maryland Commission on Artistic Property of the State Archives and Hall of Records Commission for the Maryland Heritage Committee. September 1984.

Hastings, George E. *The Life and Works of Francis Hopkinson*. Chicago: University of Chicago Press, 1926.

Irish Department of Foreign Affairs. "Ireland: The National Flag, Emblem and Anthem." Facts Sheet 7/82, Dublin.

Jaffe, Irma B. *John Trumbull: Patriot-Artist of the American Revolution*. Boston: New York Graphic Society, 1975.

Library of Congress, *Journals of the Continental Congress: 1774-1789*. Vols 18 and 21. Washington: Government Printing Office, 1910.

Lord, Walter. *The Dawn's Early Light*. New York: W.W. Norton & Co., Inc., 1972.

Mastai, Boleslaw and Marie-Louise D'Otrange. *The Stars and the Stripes*. 1st ed. New York: Alfred A. Knopf, Inc., 1973.

Mead, Hilary P. *Sea Flags -- Their General Use*. Glascow: Brown, Son and Ferguson, Ltd., Nautical Publishers, 1939.

Morgan, John Hill. *Paintings by John Trumbull at Yale Univer-*

sity of Historic Scenes and Personages Prominent in the American Revolution. New Haven: Yale University Press, 1926.

National Archives. *Papers of the Continental Congress.* Item Nos. 19, 37, 62, 78, 136, and 137.

New Zealand Embassy. "Flags of New Zealand" (fact sheet). Washington, D.C., December 1960.

Patterson, Richard S. and Richardson Dougall. *The Eagle and the Shield: A History of the Great Seal of the United States.* Washington: U.S. Government Printing Office, 1978.

Perkins, Dexter and Glyndon G. Van Deusen. *The United States of America: A History.* New York: The Macmillan Company, 1968.

Perrin, William Gordon. *British Flags, Their Early History, and Their Development at Sea, etc.* Cambridge: the University Press, 1922.

Preble, George Henry. *History of the Flag of the United States of America, etc.,* 3rd ed. Boston: James R. Osgood and Company, 1882.

Quaife, Milo M., Melvin F. Weig and Roy E. Appleman. *The History of the United States Flag: From the Revolution to the Present, Including a Guide to Its Use and Display,* 2nd ed. New York: Harper & Row, 1961.

Richardson, Edward W. *Standards and Colors of the American Revolution.* Philadelphia: University of Pennsylvania Press & The Pennsylvania Society of Sons of the Revolution and Its Color Guard, 1982.

Ridley, Jasper. *The History of England.* London: Routledge & Kegan Paul, Ltd., 1981.

Rollo, Vera F. *Maryland Personality Parade.* Lanham, Md.: Maryland Historical Press, 1970.

Schaun, George and Virginia Schaun. "Pickersgill, Mrs. Mary

Young." *The Greenberry Series on Maryland.* Vol. 5. Annapolis: Greenberry Publications, January 1967.

Sellers, Charles Coleman. *The Artist of the Revolution: The Early Life of Charles Willson Peale.* Vol. I. Philadelphia: The American Philosophical Society, 1947.

-----. *Charles Willson Peale.* New York: Charles Scribner's Sons, 1969.

Sheads, Scott. *The Rockets' Red Glare.* Centreville, Md.: Tidewater Publishers, 1986.

Smith, Whitney. *The Flag Book of the United States,* rev. ed. New York: William Morrow & Company, Inc., 1975.

Swan, Conrad. *Canada: Symbols of Sovereignty.* Toronto: University of Toronto Press, 1977.

Time, the Weekly Magazine -- Special 1776 Issue, Vol. 105, No. 20 (1975).

Trumbull, John. *The Autobiography of John Trumbull: Patriot-Artist, 1756-1843.* Edited by Theodore Sizer. New Haven: Yale University Press, 1953.

United States Code, Title 4, Chapter 1, Sections 1-3.

United States Code, Title 36, Chapter 9, Sections 141-162.

United States Code, Title 36, Chapter 10, Sections 170-186.

United States Code, Title 38, Chapter 23, Sections 901-905.

U.S. Marine Corps. *How to Respect and Display Our Flag.* Washington: U.S. Government Printing Office, 1965.

Watterson, George. *A New Guide to Washington.* Washington: R. Farnham, 1842.

Whittier, John Greenleaf. *The Complete Poetical Works of Whittier,* ed. Horace E. Scudder. Boston: Houghton, Mifflin & Co., 1984.

Wright, Louis B. *Magna Carta and the Tradition of Liberty.* Washington: United States Capitol Historical Society and Supreme Court Historical Society, 1976.

Index